A Brief History of Delos

Véronique CHANKOWSKI

ÉCOLE FRANÇAISE D'ATHÈNES
ΓΑΛΛΙΚΗ ΣΧΟΛΗ ΑΘΗΝΩΝ

(1)

CHRONOLOGY

All dates are BC unless otherwise stated.

2500: earliest traces of occupation on Mount Kynthos on Delos.

1400–1200: Mycenaean settlement on Delos.

seventh century: composition of the *Homeric Hymn to Apollo*. Development of the cult of Apollo in the Aegean world made Delos influential.

sixth century: Naxos and Paros vied in making offerings in the Delian sanctuary of Apollo.

540–528: Peisistratos tyrant of Athens had the sanctuary of Delos purified.

ca. 525: Polycrates tyrant of Samos built a maritime empire in the Aegean and chained Rhenea to Delos.

490–479: Persian Wars. The Greeks repelled the invading Persian army.

477: Athens created the Delian League. Apollo's sanctuary served as headquarters and joint treasury of the alliance.

454: the treasury was moved to Athens and the League became the instrument of Athenian imperialism.

426: Athens had the island of Delos purified, created the festival of the *Delia* and had the Temple of the Athenians built.

405: Athens defeated in the Peloponnesian War.

377: new Greek military alliance under Athenian command (or second Athenian League).

fourth century: Athens had the Temple of Pythian Apollo built on Delos.

338–336: the Greek cities, defeated by King Philip II of Macedonia, joined a military alliance under his authority.

334–323: Alexander the Great, son of Philip of Macedonia, conquered the Persian Empire, then died in Babylon.

314: Antigonos the One-Eyed, former leader of Alexander the Great's army, freed Delos from Athenian tutelage.

305: the Diadochi, former companions in arms of Alexander the Great, proclaimed themselves kings and ratified the division of the conquered lands. Birth of the Hellenistic kingdoms.

228–205: initial Roman military forays into Greece.

ca. 190: the cult of Serapis recognized by the city-state of Delos.

189: Peace of Apamea after the defeat of the Seleucid kingdom by Rome.

168: the Roman Senate placed Delos under the rule of Athens again.

ca. 150: founding of the association of the Poseidoniasts of Berytos on Delos.

146: Rome's victory in the Achaean War and destruction of Corinth.

129: creation of the Roman province of Asia after the kingdom of Pergamon was left to Rome.

88–84: First Mithridatic War between Rome and Mithridates VI, king of Pontus.

88: troops of Mithridates VI plundered Delos and slaughtered the Italians.

69: Athenodoros, a pirate in the pay of King Mithridates VI, ransacked Delos. The Roman legate Caius Triarius had a rampart erected.

67: Pompey's war against the pirates.

58: the Gabinia–Calpurnia law exempted Delos from tax levies by publicans*.

31: Octavian defeated Mark Antony at Actium to become sole master of the Roman Empire.

27: Octavian, as Emperor Augustus, organized the Roman province of Achaea.

Introduction

The remains on Delos became known to fifteenth-century seafarers and travellers and were then explored primarily by the French School at Athens from 1873 onwards. They have yielded substantial records that serve as a benchmark in Mediterranean archaeology. In conjunction with many ancient texts, they provide an outstanding account of the changing features of a civilization – its religion and institutions, its economy and everyday life – from the onset of archaic times through to late antiquity.

Lying in the heart of the Cyclades, Delos shares with other islands in the archipelago a semi-arid climate and low relief where powerful northerly and southerly winds contend or alternate. Measuring just 3.5 km^2 in area, it might seem quite insignificant had it not become, from antiquity and for several centuries, one of the Greek world's leading centres of political, religious and financial power. For visitors sailing from Mykonos along the craggy northern shore of Delos, the contrast with the haunting remains of the ancient port and sanctuaries that come into view shortly after is striking. It is that same contrast between the island's seemingly barren ground and its fabulous wealth that the myths and legends about Delos sought to explain.

The great sanctuary of Apollo that arose on the island was the hub of things. All areas of Delian life depended on it, whatever the changes down the centuries. From the earliest known developments on the island in the seventh century BC up until it was gradually deserted in the sixth century AD, through the remains we can contemplate the unique history of an island community amid the swirls and eddies of the major changes in the eastern Mediterranean.

(2)

Legends and signs

Known to Odysseus in *The Odyssey*, celebrated in the hymns of the poets from the archaic period to the Hellenistic period, listed among the grand designs of Alexander the Great, and coveted by the Romans in their conquest of the Mediterranean, Delos was a constant concern of the major powers until it was again lost from sight – *Delos adelos* in the famous wordplay of antiquity. A tiny and yet prestigious centre of power in the Mediterranean: this is the paradox explored by the legends and myths about the island.

Delos is evoked in the verse of the *Homeric Hymn to Apollo*, probably written down in the second half of the seventh century to be sung at religious festivals. Before expounding the god's great deeds at Delphi and in other places in Greece, the poem sets down in writing the legend of the birth of Apollo and Artemis on Delos.

Their mother Leto, daughter of a titan, with child by Zeus, scours the Earth as a fugitive because all its peoples refuse refuge to her, fearing the wrath of Zeus' lawful wife, Hera. Leto promises the small forgotten island of Delos great prosperity if it accepts to let her bear her children there: "Delos, if you would be willing to be the abode of my son Phoebus Apollo and make him a rich temple —; for no other will touch you, as you will find: and I think you will never be rich in oxen and sheep, nor bear vintage nor yet produce plants abundantly. But if you have the temple of far-shooting Apollo, all men will bring you hecatombs* and gather here, and incessant savour of rich sacrifice will always arise, and you will feed those who dwell in you from the hand of strangers; for truly your own soil is not rich" (v. 51–60, transl. H.G. Evelyn-White). In answer to the tiny island's qualms, Leto even swore an oath in the name of her unborn son: "and you he shall honour above all" (v. 88). The birth accomplished the miracle immediately: "Then with gold all Delos [was laden, beholding the child of Zeus and Leto, for joy because the god chose her above the islands and shore to make his dwelling in her …] blossomed as does a mountain-top with woodland flowers" (v. 135–139).

In the third century, as part of the poetic renewal of the Hellenistic period, the *Hymn to Apollo* by the poet Callimachus worked several variants into the legend while taking up the gist of the initial narrative, accounting for the unexpected prosperity of Delos. At that date, as inscriptions and archaeology reveal, the arid island did indeed see cattle graze the land and vines grow, while crowds thronged around the smoke of sacrifices and money was plentiful because of the prestige of Apollo's sanctuary.

These legends were associated with actual places on the island. The lake over which swans flew heralding the birth of the divine twins, the palm tree beneath which the birth occurred, Mount Kynthos (105), the highest point on the island, where the youthful Artemis trained as a huntress, the altar of horns that the boy Apollo built were all "places of remembrance" and relics designed to illustrate the finer points of the legendary narrative. Ancient pilgrims or visitors could admire them as they went through the sanctuary, seeing for themselves that this sacred story was authentic.

(3)

The development of Delos thus appears to be intimately related to the figure of the god Apollo, as archaeology confirms. Before the seventh century, the island was occupied by various communities: the earliest traces of settlement, identified on Mount Kynthos, date from 2500 and were those of pre-Hellenic populations. In Mycenaean times, between 1400 and 1200, the island accommodated a settlement along with graves and places of worship. But that presence, of which very little is known, remained modest compared with the growth observed from the seventh century onwards. This suggests that it was the development of the cult of Apollo in the Aegean Sea area from the onset of the archaic period, as attested by *The Hymn to Apollo*, that made Delos into a religious centre that little by little became unrivalled.

The community of Delians, "a sacred people"

The Delian population settled beside the sanctuary from which it drew its prestige and prosperity. Sharing was no easy matter: the cramped territory had to provide both for the local population's economic activities and for congregations at the great sanctuary. Even so, the situation worked to the advantage of the Delians, who derived many benefits from it, leading to them being both envied and mocked by other Greeks in antiquity. By a tradition that was well attested in the

Hellenistic period, the Delians were called "parasites of the god", as a reflection of their special standing. The *parasitos* is one who eats at his benefactor's table and the god Apollo did indeed "feed" the Delians in various ways. Throughout their history, the community of Delians benefitted from the sanctuary's wealth and from the sacred territory being inviolable, and so they were sheltered from the economic, social and military hardships that beset ordinary city-states. The Delians themselves signalled their special status by claiming to be "a sacred people". The term indicated their enjoyment of the exceptional standing that fell to all the land that Apollo was considered to own as tutelary divinity. The expression is first recorded by the historian Herodotus (*Histories*, VI, 97) who tells how the Persian invader spared the sanctuary of Delos because its inhabitants were *hieroi* ("holy men"). The Greek world's acknowledgement of the sacred character of Delian territory came about over time, especially through the string of episodes of outside rule it experienced. For its part, the Delian community

(4, 5)

The community of Delians, "a sacred people"

constantly gave shape to this sacred standing through the transparency of its economic system, with the sanctuary's accounting records carved in stone, and through active diplomacy to defend the island's inviolable character, as a number of inscriptions attest.

The circumstances of the neighbouring island of Rhenea were likewise complex. Being consecrated in part at least to Apollo, it was in some sense an extension of Delian territory. The necropolis of Delos was laid out there, as was a sanctuary of Artemis and various farmsteads. And yet, the city-state of Rhenea struggled through over the centuries, across the narrows off the west coast of its cumbersome Delian neighbour.

The city-state of Delos probably grew around the sanctuary from archaic times, with traces of settlement of the classical period having been found in the future location of the "Theatre District". It is primarily the public monuments that give us a glimpse of its layout. Beside the sanctuary, to the east of the main plain, several buildings from the classical period attest to the Delians' civic institutions: an *ekklesiasterion** (47) where the Assembly of the people gathered, possibly a *bouleuterion** (21) for the public records and Council meetings, and a prytaneion* (22) for the business of the magistrates.

While fulfilling their responsibilities with respect to the island's main cult, that of the "Apollonian triad" (Apollo, Artemis, Leto), the Delians did not fail to honour other deities of the Greek pantheon, beginning with the quarrelsome Hera, whose sanctuary (101) stood on a terrace at the foot of Mount Kynthos, and Aphrodite, for whom a small neighbourhood sanctuary (88) can be seen north-west of the theatre. It was constructed thanks to the generosity of a great Delian family whose statutes once flanked the entrance to the small temple.

Associated with the cult of Apollo and Dionysos, the theatre (114), which was monumentalized in the course of the third century, attests to the cultural activities of the community that was very much open to influences from outside. But the Delians also paid worship to their founding hero Anios Archegetes in the Archegesion, which stood in what was probably a district of the Hellenistic city in the centre of the island (74). Two lintels bearing inscriptions belonging to this sanctuary prohibited non-Delians from entering; evidence of a local and identity-based cult in deliberate contrast with the cosmopolitan nature of the sanctuaries of the plain.

From the sixth to the second centuries, dedications, decrees and the very many administrative acts cut in stone preserve the memory of some five thousand Delian names, for which, in most instances, we can trace the families over several

(6)

generations together with their occupations. A good number of them held magistracies and civic responsibilities within a community that probably never exceeded seven to eight thousand inhabitants. A few monuments that can be seen on the site indicate the identity of these Delian families. For example, just before crossing the propylaea* ⑤, a large exedra* can be seen bearing several inscriptions in a script typical of the third century. It is a family monument, signed by a Corinthian sculptor, Aristophilos son of Eusthenes. On the exedra

(7)

wall, two dedications reveal there were statues in the likeness of a Delian family: "Soteles son of Telemnestos dedicated the statue of his son Telemnestos to the gods" (left, *IG* XI 4, 1173) and "Soteles son of Telemnestos dedicated the statue of his wife Xenaino to the gods" (centre, *IG* XI 4, 1174). This same Soteles is known from several other inscriptions attesting to him holding various public offices: notably he was archon and organized votes on a number of decrees in the People's Assembly. By way of recognition, the Delian people dedicated a statute to him, whose base is to the right of the exedra (*IG* XI 4, 1086).

Alongside these various offices, the inscriptions and remains tell us of craftsmen, shopkeepers, growers, livestock farmers, fishermen and businessmen. Beyond the area taken up by the sanctuaries stretched the *chora** of Delos with its farmland dotted with farmsteads, several of which have been identified by archaeologists, and its man-made terraces for crops, laid out as far **(8)** back as the fifth century at least. And yet the Delian population, protected by its sanctuary, was constantly subjected to the influence, competition or even rule of powers which, from archaic times to Roman times, saw in Apollo's sanctuary a prime location for displaying their sway over the Aegean. It is, besides, to this string of powers that the island of Delos owes most of its buildings.

The archaic period: Delos, showcase of the maritime powers

The stone lions, clearly visible to visitors walking through the sanctuary, were probably among the earliest spectacular consecrations of the plain in the course of the seventh century. They line an avenue that must have led to one of the sanctuary's entrances.

These statues of Naxos marble with their stylized wiry bodies were a monumental offering erected on Delos by the Naxians, who also contributed to the sanctuary's expansion through other constructions: numerous statues of *kouroi** and *korai**, offerings to Apollo depicting youths and maidens, that must have stood within the sanctuary's precincts; plus a long building referred to from antiquity as (9)

the "oikos* of the Naxians" ⑥, displaying all the characteristics of Naxian architecture of the archaic period. It was probably not a temple but a treasury for offerings, its use being attested by epigraphy a few centuries after it was built. A colossal *kouros* statue 9 m high, known as the "Colossus of the Naxians" stood beside it. Only the torso and pelvis can be seen today next to the monument, along with the huge base ⑨ with inscriptions on two sides: one bears a dedication from the archaic period ("I am of the same stone, statue and pedestal"), and the other a Naxian dedication engraved in classical times ("the Naxians to Apollo"). Sculpted in the early sixth century, this ensemble was famed back in antiquity as a feat of artistry.

Other works from Naxos can be seen in the Delian sanctuary and display, both through their figured elements and the text of the dedication, the know-how of its sculptors: the base of Euthykartides, which bears an archaic signature written in *boustrophedon** (Delos Museum) or the statue of a feminine character named Nikandre in the dedication in hexameters (National Archaeological Museum, Athens). Another neighbouring island famed for its marble productions, Paros, the artistic rival to Naxos in the sixth century, was not to be outdone and also decked the Delian sanctuary with statues characteristic of its style.

Archaeologists and historians have long debated what this Naxian and Parian artistic presence on Delos meant. Should it be construed as territorial and political dominion over the island or even over the surrounding Cyclades? The historian Thucydides, in attempting in the *History of the Peloponnesian War* to explain the development of Athenian imperialism in the fifth century, was the first to emphasize how important the sanctuary of Delos was for maritime empires. He claimed that control of the Aegean seemed inseparable from hold over the sanctuary of Apollo on Delos. In giving several examples of thalassocracies* that preceded the Athenian Empire, Thucydides was mindful to emphasize the part played by the cult of Delian Apollo: in the latter half of the sixth century, the tyrant* Polycrates of Samos, who conquered an Aegean maritime empire, seized the island of Rhenea which lies next to Delos and consecrated it to Delian Apollo by chaining it to Delos; or the tyrant of Athens Peisistratos, who extended his influence in the Cyclades to the point of setting up the tyrant Lygdamis on Naxos and purifying the island of Delos between 546 and 528 by having all the graves within sight of the sanctuary removed.

It was in archaic times that Athens imposed its presence on Delos through the construction of a temple, referred to in the inscriptions as the *porinos naos* or "porous stone temple", the foundations of which can be seen in the centre of the sacred precinct (11). This practice was maintained down the centuries since the same space continued in Hellenistic times to be the prime spot for Mediterranean kings and city-states to express their power through votive monuments whose dedications recorded the donors' names and titles. But at the time Athens, after its victories in the wars with the Medes, gained ascendancy over the other Greek city-states, it displayed more especially its ties with the sanctuary of Delian Apollo and made its mark there like no other power in the history of Delos.

(11)

The classical period: Delos as an instrument of Athenian imperialism

Although the sanctuary of Delos was established by 478–477 as the meeting point for the allies of the Delian League and the place where its treasury was kept, this status was short-lived. The growing might of Athens which took on the form of an increasingly imperialistic power, the *arche* Thucydides describes in the *History of the Peloponnesian War*, put an end to the federal complexion of the initial league, probably by 454. Yet Delos remained no less a central feature in the imperial ideology of Athens, which sought to impose its rule over the (12)

island of Apollo that was so strategically located in the Aegean Sea. Being sacred territory, Delos was not subject to any military occupation. It is the inscriptions that attest in great detail to the nature of Athenian power there.

From the fifth century onwards, a statement of the sanctuary's property was carved annually in the form of great stelae recording administrative acts. The stelae, often a metre or more high, were exhibited in the sanctuary, possibly between the "Temple of the Athenians" as it was called (12), built around 425, and the Great Temple (13), begun around 475 and only completed in the early third century. The passageway between the two buildings was lined with a series of bases in which the tall stelae could be inserted. These stelae yield highly detailed evidence about the development of the administration of Apollo's sanctuary under the Athenians, who sent boards of magistrates – sometimes every five years, sometimes annually – to oversee the management of the god's property, with the Delians holding subordinate offices. Aristotle, or at any rate the Aristotelean author of the *Constitution of the Athenians* (LXII, 2), refers to them explicitly by the title of amphictyons*, which is found in the inscriptions of the classical period. These teams of administrators, in charge of all the economic and financial business generated by the sanctuary, had detailed accounts carved that enlighten certain aspects of Delian history. These administrative acts bear witness to the renting to individuals of farmland and buildings belonging to the sanctuary, and taxes collected by Apollo's treasury for the use of various harbour infrastructures. The Athenian administration thereby developed a model for the management of sacred property, very much like that observed in the written documents of the sanctuaries of Attica, that made it possible to build up cash reserves and meet major expenses such as the repair of buildings, new construction work and costly festivals like the *Delia*, that were the Aegean counterpart of the Panathenaea of Athens, for the glory of the imperialistic city-state. Moreover, to improve the yield from the god's capital and property holdings, the Athenian administrators introduced a system of interest-bearing loans, not just for individual customers but also for the island city-states. The income from the interest payments financed spending to enhance Athenian prestige. Substantial amounts were handled: in the fourth century, more than 10 talents* were in regular circulation in the form of loans.

In this way, the Athenians laid down an economic system based on the meticulous and rational exploitation of Apollo's wealth. These same management principles were found in the following centuries and, when it came down to it, ensured the Delians' prosperity. Right from the classical period, the Delians were the main beneficiaries of the supply of rental property and credit organized by the Athenian administration. This system also meant capital could circulate in the island city-states that borrowed from the sanctuary. The money in circulation, Athenian currency, could be used in all the circuits of Mediterranean-wide trade. The development of the Athenian administration on Delos was a venture in managing Apollo's property in the service of Athenian rule over the Aegean world that was exercised virtually undivided. It proved remarkably continuous from the fifth to the fourth centuries, barring a very brief few years when, further to the Athenian defeat of 405 in the Peloponnesian War, Sparta showed some interest in Delos. Apollo's sanctuary thus underwent substantial expansion in the classical period that also reflected the prestige and power of Athens.

The imperialistic city-state made its religious and cultural mark on the island by trying to eradicate or attenuate any overly specific Delian features. In the course of the fourth century, the construction of the temple of Pythian Apollo between the Artemision and the famed Horn Altar, or the highlighting of the part played by the Athenian hero Theseus in the mythical history of Delos, clearly reflected Athens' intention to redirect the island's religious practices under its authority. Yet Athenian rule over the island ultimately had to come to terms with the continuation of the Delian city-state, after Athens had sought in vain to use the argument of ritual purity to expel the island's inhabitants from what was declared holy ground. A century after the purification at the instigation of Peisistratos, the Athenians set about a yet more radical purification, related by Thucydides (*History of the Peloponnesian* War, III, 104, 1, transl. R. Warner): "In the same winter the Athenians, no doubt because of some oracle, carried out ceremonies of purification on Delos. In former times the tyrant Pisistratus also had purified the island, though not the whole of it – only as much of it as could be seen from the temple. On the present occasion, however, the whole island was purified in the following way. All the tombs of those who had died in Delos were dug up, and it was proclaimed that in future no deaths or births were to be allowed in the island; those who were about to die or to give birth were to be carried across to Rhenea…". Immediately afterwards, the Athenians introduced the great festival of the *Delia* under their patronage and expelled the Delians in 422–421. The following year, with support from the oracle of Delphi, the Delians managed to secure their resettlement in their homeland. The Delian population was probably divided over what attitude to take towards Athenian rule. Many local families held administrative functions in the management of the sanctuary's property in the fifth and fourth centuries. Some were commercial and financial associates of Athenians. But other Delians opposed the authority established over Apollo's sanctuary, resorting both to violence and to the courts of law. Administrative records report a trial for an attack on Athenian magistrates who were thrown out of the sanctuary by a few Delians in 376. Several literary sources also mention a lawsuit, in confused circumstances, supposedly opposing Athens and Delos in the court of the Delphian amphictiony* over the administration of the sanctuary in the mid-fourth century.

Although Athenian domination was challenged by some of the population, Athens' influence also pervaded Delian institutions and political culture. Evidence of this was the construction of the civic building of the prytaneion (22), flanked by a herm whose head atop a pillar is plainly visible from the harbour. This was a thoroughly Athenian tradition.

When it comes down to it, the Delian civic community was constantly striving for independence in its own land and, by the same token, recognition of its capacity to administer the great sanctuary of Apollo there on its own. It was probably in this complex context of Athenian rule, and because of the island's sacred status, that the Delians' political consciousness was forged, making neutrality the guiding principle of their strategic outlook.

(16)

The period of the Hellenistic kings: Delos as an arena for competing powers

The history of Delos can only be understood in conjunction with the major upheavals in Mediterranean history. In the late fourth century, Athens' domination of the Aegean ebbed with the rise of other powers. The development of the kingdom of Macedonia under Philip II, then its expansion to the Orient against the Persian Empire under his son Alexander profoundly transformed the Greek world which, with the advent of the Hellenistic kingdoms further to the death of Alexander the Great in 323, moved up an order of magnitude. In this Greek world now extended to the Orient and Egypt, Delos and its sanctuary continued to play a decisive part in the centre of the Aegean.

These transformations had two major consequences. First, the eclipse of Athens enabled the Delians to recover full sovereignty over their territory and the administration of Apollo's sanctuary by way of the great territorial shifts that came about under the new Greco-Macedonian warlords, (17) the Diadochi, who were to become the Hellenistic kings a few years later. This opened up for Delos, as of the year 314, a period that historians today call the "Independence".

Second, in line with what had happened in earlier times, Apollo's sanctuary became a prestigious showcase for the new Hellenistic powers and many works of art were exhibited there. The political neutrality displayed by the Delian city-state facilitated the show of strength by rival powers in the Aegean Sea for domination over new territories, and those powers exhibited the monuments to their victories in the sanctuary.

A number of constructions along the avenue from the propylaea to the temples of Apollo are evidence of this. At the corner of the Temple of the Athenians, a large blue marble base 8 m long paid homage to Philetairos, the founder of the Attalid dynasty of Pergamon, after his death in 263 ⑩. The monument must have included a sculpted group that has disappeared, but the verse dedication that can still be read on the base gives all the necessary indications:

"O blest Philetairos, our lord who for godlike poets/And skilful modellers shows equal care;/These proclaim your great power, the first with hymns,/The others with display of the skill of their hands./Since once you brought swift Ares against the Celts, unlucky in war,/And drove them far beyond your land's frontiers,/These choice works of Nikeratos did Sosikrates/Set up for you, in sea-girt Delos,/As a memorial, famous in song; and not even Hephaistos himself,/Beholding their art would censure it." (*IG* 11.4.1105. Transl. in A. Stewart, *One Hundred Greek Sculptors, Their Careers and Extant Works;* Perseus Digital Library)

Other monuments on Delos bear witness to the great successes of the Attalid kings in repelling the Galatians (Celts), like the equestrian statue of Epigenes, general of King Attalus I, and another Attalid monument, whose inscribed bases remain in front of the colonnade lining the Agora of the Delians ㊸, or the statues found again in the Agora of the Italians ㊼.

The notoriety of the Delian sanctuary made it a prime venue for passing out information. A number of edicts and international treaties were carved and exhibited in the great sanctuaries of the Greek world, of which Delos was one. The Antigonid kings were probably those who used Apollo's sanctuary most to

A Brief History of Delos

commemorate their victories and the development of their alliances, especially when faced with the rising power of Rome in the years 180–170.

Delos also benefitted from the euergetism* of the Hellenistic kings, soon imitated by other non-Greek kingdoms, who embellished the sanctuary with new constructions and came to give it its current layout. The main avenues leading to the religious buildings of the central plain are lined to this day by countless inscribed bases that are evidence of the acts of dedication of statutes and votive objects. Offered to the god Apollo or to the Apollonian triad (Apollo, Artemis, Leto), they are as much a display of the piety of the dedicants as of their eagerness to be seen in a prestigious location frequented by populations from far and wide. Porticoes were erected to line the main throughfares. In the course of the third century, through the generosity of several Hellenistic kings, Delos saw its harbour area wholly transformed by the addition of urban amenities that meant it could cope with the surge in Mediterranean trade. Skirting the *dromos**, the possibly Attalid South Portico ④ cut off the Agora of the Delians from the harbour area in the mid-third century. Then a few decades later, the portico of the Antigonid king of Macedonia Philip V, the dedication of which is visible on the monument, closed off the space, before the perspective was completed by a third portico backing on to the previous one and facing the sea ③. Running along the northern side of the sanctuary, the Portico of Antigonos Gonatas,

built in the latter half of the third century ㉙, served a similar purpose. On the island, athletic infrastructures that served for the great Delian festivals also benefitted from gifts from Hellenistic kings: a lintel of the xystus, the covered gallery where athletes could train, behind the stadium, bears an inscription naming its donator, the Lagid king Ptolemy IX, around 110.

The Delians, now in charge of the administration of the sacred site, developed a policy based on neutrality and devoted to preserving the sanctuary's interests, which were likewise those of the entire city-state. The very numerous inscriptions for the period, and in particular the honorific decrees voted for by the Delian institutions, bear witness to the great adaptive capacity of the new generations of islanders who became masters in Mediterranean international relations. The sanctuary's accounts record several instances of spending on honorific crowns*, credited to the city-state. They were intended as prestigious honours paid to the great powers of the Hellenistic world as circumstances dictated. The Attalid kings Attalus I and Eumenes II, the Seleucid Antiochos III and his consort Laodike, the Antigonids Philip V and Perseus, along with other sovereigns like Prusias of Bithynia and Massinissa of Numidia, together with the Rhodian People, the Aetolian League and the Senate and People of Rome as of the 170s were all beneficiaries.

Several monuments still in place tell us of this diplomatic activity. For example, a seemingly unspectacular base carried the statue of a figure whose identity is revealed by the inscribed dedication: "Hermon son of Solon consecrated the statue of King Massinissa son of King Gaia, his friend, to Apollo. Polianthes made the statue."

Celebrated unifier of Numidia, staged by Corneille in his tragedy *Sophonisba*, and ally of the Roman Scipio Africanus against Carthage, Delos hosted several statues of Massinissa. This one was consecrated by a Delian, Hermon son of Solon, whose name is recorded in the island's accounts for having arranged the sale of more than 1000 quintals of wheat presented by Massinissa in 180 for the benefit of the Delian city-state with the support of Rhodes. In this dedication, he calls himself "friend" of the king, probably a courtly title as evidence of the workings of local diplomacy: the Delians managed to secure many advantages for their city-state through the connections of their influential fellow-citizens with the great Mediterranean powers. As for the sculptor Polianthes, he signed other statues on Delos that tell us he was from Cyrene.

Independent Delos as a Hellenistic city-state

Taking up the Athenians' methods for administering finances, Delian magistrates, named *"hieropoioi"*, acting collegially and now on an annual basis, took on the many tasks of managing the sacred space: letting out Apollo's land and properties, collecting farm rents, property rents and taxes, arranging interest-bearing loans, making inventories of and maintaining the collections of offerings along with organizing worksites for the upkeep and renovation of the sanctuary or the construction of new monuments, financing religious festivals and contests that drew in audiences from various Mediterranean city-states.

This intense activity in managing the god's property was one of the major tasks that mobilized the Delian civic community, who were both devoted to and had an interest in preserving a sacred heritage from which they derived their prosperity. In this, the city-state of Delos acquired and displayed considerable skill in public administration, both through the annual activity of the boards of magistrates and in the meetings of the Council and the Assembly of the People, tasked with many financial decisions. Close on five hundred administrative acts, accounts and inventories of the property of Apollo's sanctuary are evidence of this. Continuing the tradition laid down by the Athenians in classical times, the huge stelae often more than 1 m in height were still carved and exhibited in the sanctuary so as to set before the eyes of all the particulars of the management operations performed annually for the god's account.

The stelae were engraved on both faces and sometimes on the edges, so much data was there to be recorded. This open access to accounting information, duly approved and validated by the city-state's institutions, was both a guarantee of the probity of the Delian community in managing the sanctuary and the display of an administrative and financial feat, the methods of which owed much to the Athenian innovations of the classical period.

The Delians, "parasites" of Apollo, acted with devotion with regard to the sacred heritage but benefited in equal measure from sharing the island with the sanctuary. The city-state of Delos had its own resources that garnished

a public treasury, although far outweighed by Apollo's wealth. However, the city-state could draw on the sanctuary's cash holdings as a permanent credit line, which it refunded over the course of the year from its own tax income. The sacred character of the whole of the island meant that, via the sanctuary, it could finance the construction and maintenance of public buildings such as the theatre completed in the course of the third century or the great Hypostyle Hall ⑤⓪ erected near the harbour at the very end of the third century. It was an immense administrative and commercial building whose architrave* of the south colonnade bore the dedication of the Delians (*Delioi*). These were non-negligible advantages compared with other city-states in the Greek world for which several sources show the efforts they had to put into collecting the cash needed for their grain supply, construction work and defence of their land.

Apollo's sanctuary must have looked like one great building site: contractors, craftsmen, warehousemen and merchants rubbed shoulders with pilgrims within the sacred precinct and throughout the island, where the pace of activity was just as frenetic as that of the ritual acts and sacrifices. The sanctuary's records of account, by documenting payments for construction and repair work on the various buildings covered by the sacred treasury, tell us of a large number of craftsmen, trades and specialities. The archaeological remains confirm the scale of artisanal activity on Delos, including for later periods.

Protected from warfare by the island being inviolable because sacred and protected from financial hardship by Apollo's treasury, the Delians also profited from the sanctuary's drawing power in their commercial dealings, which they conducted on the island and in various ports around the Aegean Sea. The most influential of them were partners in Mediterranean-wide business networks. However, they were soon to come into competition, when not united by shared interests and profits, with traders of the eastern Mediterranean who, in the mid-third century, judging from the evidence of the sanctuary's accounting records, forced their way into Aegean maritime circuits. Sources attest to the role of *emporion** that Delos played in the Aegean Sea from the fourth century onwards. Wheat trading circuits (21)

in the eastern Mediterranean, from Egypt, Sicily and the Black Sea, probably found a redistribution centre on Delos from the beginning of the Hellenistic period. This role developed steadily throughout the third and second centuries to the point that the island gradually became a cosmopolitan centre and a reflection of the Hellenistic civilization of the eastern Mediterranean.

From the late fourth century onwards, the neighbouring islands were grouped into an island league, the Nesiotic *koinon*, under the patronage of the Antigonids, then the Lagids, and then under the influence

(22)

of Rhodes. The interests of the consortium probably extended beyond the religious sphere: although the *koinon* exhibited its honorific decrees in Apollo's sanctuary, it probably also enabled the organization of commercial networks and the preservation of regional interests in the economic circuits involving Delos. The Delian economy came to terms with the shifts in Hellenistic power in the Aegean Sea. Being close to the Lagids when they extended their influence against the Antigonids in the Cyclades until the mid-third century, Delos set itself up as a hub for the grain trade. It also turned towards Rhodes, an independent city-state and great trading power, to the extent of gradually reducing the weight of its own coinage to become aligned with Rhodian monetary practices.

A number of laws and decrees attest to the Delian city-state's readiness to take on both its role in organizing business by cosmopolitan trading circles in its territory and its duties to protect the interests of its own citizens. One such record can still be seen in the old harbour area, inside the portico built later on the spot. It is a third-century law governing the sale of wood and charcoal, two strategic supplies for the Aegean islands that were lacking in them and for the (23) trading networks that derived sizeable profits through speculation in them. The

whole purpose of the law was to regulate the trade without harming either business circles or consumers. However, Delian independence could not withstand the far-reaching changes in the Greek world. Although protected by its active diplomacy with regard to the Hellenistic kings to whom it accorded honour and privileges in the sanctuary by playing on the geopolitical rivalries among conquerors, the tiny city-state of Delos was helpless against the gradual collapse of the great kingdoms of the eastern Mediterranean in the course of the second century and the growing power of Rome. Having long had contacts with Greece and being amenable to its cultural influences, Rome supported Athens in the Aegean Sea from the second century onwards, backing its ambitions for a renaissance. Athens, crushed by

A Brief History of Delos

Macedonian domination in the course of the third century, saw this new alliance as a chance to restore an earlier position when its rule over the island of Apollo ensured it of a central position in the Aegean Sea. In the territorial reorganization following the victory of Roman consul Lucius Aemilius Paullus against King Perseus in the Third Macedonian War, it was probably by heeding Athenian claims that the Roman Senate decided on a far-reaching transformation in the status of the island of Delos in 167. The land was placed again under Athenian tutelage and exonerated from taxes. There followed a period of conflict between Athens and the Delians, attested to by the historian Polybius; it ended with the Delians being expelled definitively and their city-state discontinued.

Although the Roman decision of 167 was a catastrophe for the Delians, many of whom settled on the neighbouring island of Rhenea and others in Achaea, it fitted with the earlier periods in several respects. Fiscally, the status of the free port merely extended an existing state of affairs: since the fourth century the Delian city-state had conceded very many tax exemptions to entrepreneurs and traders, thereby setting itself up as a central marketplace in Aegean trade. As for the Athenians, they saw their domination of the island as a restoration of their (24) earlier rights: the administrators who were sent straight away to Delos had as their first mission to perform a full audit of the sacred property, including the monetary assets, buildings, amenities and offerings.

Independent Delos as a Hellenistic city-state

Delos under Rome's tutelage: Athens' share, between religious traditions and economic deal-making

Athens' resumption of control over the sacred island was reflected by the great city-state making its mark on the sanctuary: the dedication on the Hypostyle Hall ⑤ was altered to feature the name of the Athenians (*Athenaioi*), who also had their own dedication carved on the new propylaea. Several families of note settled on Delos: the family of the spouses Dioskourides and Kleopatra is known to us from the dedication of a statuary group in their likeness, the original of which is in Delos Museum and a copy on site, in one of the houses ㉕

A Brief History of Delos

in the Theatre District. The inscription carved on the base explains the couple's intentions in the 130s:

"Kleopatra daughter of Adrastos of the deme Myrrhinous dedicated the statue of her spouse Dioskourides son of Theodoros of the deme Myrrhinous after he had consecrated the two dolphin-style silver tripods that stand in the Temple of Apollo on either side of the entrance, under the archonship of Timarchos in Athens."

Other families are known from inscriptions, dedications and inventories of offerings that attest to the Athenians' intention to advertise at great expense and through lavish objects the ties that bound them to Apollo's sacred island. These religious and social displays reflected, in Athens, a conservative undercurrent that emphasized ancestral traditions and through rituals revived ceremonies associated with Attic-Delian myths. During this period, the cult of Pythian Apollo on Delos was particularly fostered by Athens which saw in it a chance to tie together two major sanctuaries – Delphi and Delos – over which it intended to exert its influence. The Athenians also promoted festivals on Delos in honour of their hero Theseus and transformed the traditional festivals of Apollo by restoring the *Delia* of the classical period and reorganizing the *Apollonia*.

This return of Athenian rule to Delos was underpinned by new magistracies. Each year Athens delegated an *"epimeletes* of the island" to head its administration. This was plainly a prestigious office because the *epimeletai* were invariably chosen from among the great Athenian families and had often held high office as *strategoi* or archons in Athens itself. They were supported by other magistrates, annually appointed to head the various areas of Delian administration. Their offices are known to us through several inscriptions exhibited in the sanctuary: commercial matters for the *epimeletes* of the *emporion* and the *agoranomos*, sacred property for the heads of the sanctuaries, athletic institutions for the gymnasiarchs and their subordinates. The island of Delos was thus connected with the city-state of Athens as in the classical period.

On the scale of the Hellenistic world, Athens' resumed control fitted into a new political and economic context. By making Delos a free port, the Roman Senate merely confirmed and furthered the development of the island as a centre for trade in the Aegean Sea, to the detriment of the city-state of Rhodes from where, for that matter, an embassy travelled to Rome to complain of the repercussions of the Senate's decision. Athens immediately saw this as a chance to recover its economic power that Macedonian rule had stifled. The resumption of control over Delos saw Athens strike new silver coinage, the stephanephoric tetradrachm, also referred to as "wreath-bearing" coinage because of the olive wreath that now

Delos under Rome's tutelage

(26)

ringed the owl, the habitual symbol of the goddess Athena whose head was figured on the obverse of the coins. It was one of the most familiar mintages of the Greek world and circulated throughout the eastern Mediterranean. Between the mid-second and early first centuries, issues were made annually in increasing volumes.

With the stephanephoric tetradrachm, which soon became an international trading currency for the Hellenistic world, Athens was renewing with one of the ambitions of its classical imperialism: to dominate trade and commerce through currency. The weakening of Rhodes in 167, then Rome's destruction of Corinth in 146, followed by the organization of the Roman province of Asia from 129 onwards all created particularly favourable circumstances for the free port of Delos, which became the main redistributive centre in the eastern Mediterranean between Campania and the Levant. The island owed its growing wealth at the time to the grain trade, which remained one of the leading sources of profit in the Hellenistic world, and to the slave trade, with several sources testifying that slaves were brought to Delos by the shipload to be sold on to suppliers throughout the eastern Mediterranean.

Although the great Athenian families certainly benefitted from Delos to grow more prosperous through their inclusion in financial circuits, the trading activities were usually performed by Orientals* and Italians, and it was through income procured by its currency that the city-state of Athens became wealthier through Delos. But the Athenian magistrates, perhaps influenced by a Roman practice in keeping with the Greek tradition of euergetism, were eager to show their generosity – and by the same token the power of Athens over Apollo's island – by investing in the construction of commercial facilities. The action of Theophrastos, *epimeletes* of Delos in 126–125, was commemorated by a statue pedestal that can be seen in the middle of the agora whose construction he financed, along with other harbour facilities, in front of the Hypostyle Hall ⑤⓪. The dedication sets out the reasons for honouring him: "*Statue of* Theophrastos son of Herakleitos, of the deme Acharnai, former superintendent of Delos, who laid out the market place and built piers around the harbour, *dedicated* by the Athenians residing in Delos and by the Romans and other foreign merchants and shipowners resident

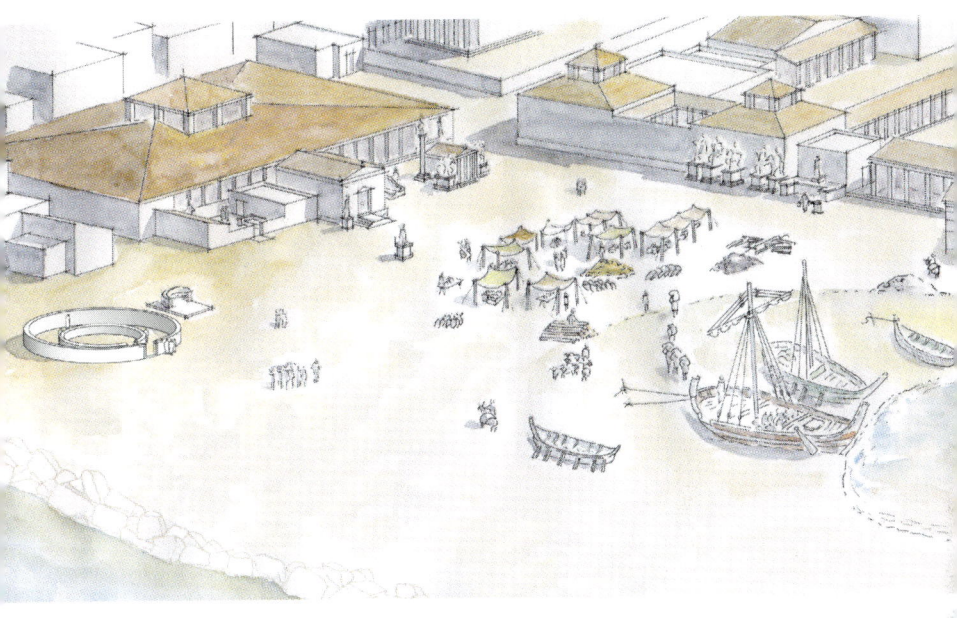

(27) in Delos, because of his goodness, his magnanimity, and his kindnesses to them" (*ID* 1645) [Attalus, transl. N. Lewis & M. Reinhold].

Delos therefore owed many of its second- and first-century developments and port facilities to Athens. Some of them have left little trace, but comparison of sources yields evidence of their importance for everyday commercial activity. This was the case, for instance, of the *kukloi* presented by one Sokrates, *agoranomos* on Delos, who, on leaving office, consecrated a circular monument to Apollo for the auctioning of slaves and wares in the Agora of Theophrastos. Curved coping stones can still be seen on the site as well as, though now swallowed by the sea, the lowermost courses of the monument, forming two concentric rings. The scale of the commercial infrastructures is clearly visible along the seafront with more than 1000 m of warehousing. This row of buildings ⟨122⟩ opening onto the dockside – though who commissioned them is unknown to us – provided storage and administrative areas and is evidence of the scope of commercial activities on Delos. Between the warehouses and the Agora of Theophrastos ⟨49⟩ another agora ⟨2⟩ was developed in front of the former square of the Delians ⟨84⟩. Named the "Agora of the Hermaists and Competaliasts" by archaeologists because of the cult monuments there and the inscriptions around it, designating Italians, it was surrounded by shops and warehouses.

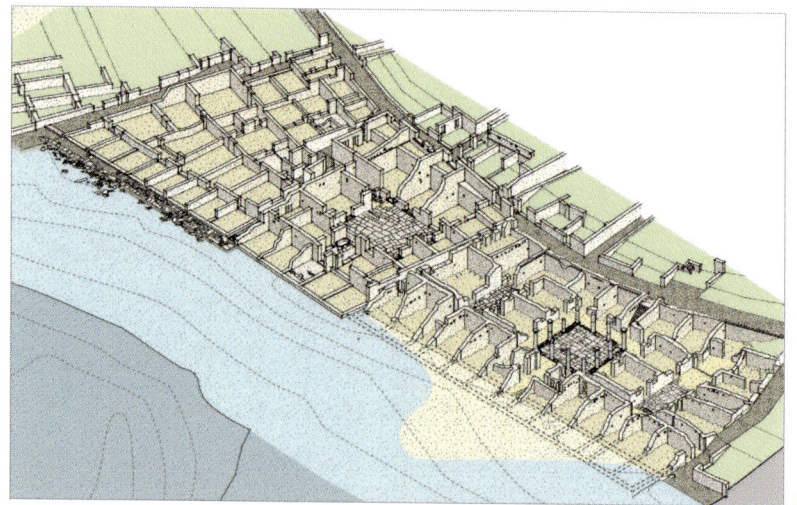

(28)

(29)

Although the Athenian administration worked towards a coherent organization of the urban area, the constructions on Delos also display the unwavering determination of the powers that vied through their offerings to hold their own on this island that was so very much coveted both for its religious influence and for its commercial advantages.

Commerce and religion on Delos: Apollo's cosmopolitan island

The inscription carved on the base of the statue of Theophrastos, like many other dedications honouring Athenian magistrates or influential politicians, paints a picture of the new society now populating Apollo's island. Businessmen passing through to make deals in the free port, Athenians, Romans and Orientals settled on Delos where they had houses built. Within a few decades, several new districts appeared in the north of the island and around the stadium ⑦⑨. Not all of them have been excavated, but those that can be seen give a glimpse of a cosmopolitan society that shared a Greek way of life. Their architecture sometimes adopted the Roman house with its atrium as a model, but not exclusively so and with many a local adaptation. On the island's east coast, in the Stadium District, a

(31)

house with an underground reservoir and several dedications to "God in the highest" suggests there was a Jewish community practising its own rites. This is corroborated by there being a synagogue (80), the earliest known outside of Palestine since it was built in the course of the first century, although well after

(32)

Commerce and religion on Delos

the first Jewish families had settled on Delos, who from the few inscriptions still visible on the shore, arrived in the first half of the second century.

The oriental traders also left traces of their presence on Delos. A residence in the "lake neighbourhood" was the premises ⑤⑦ of a club of businessmen from Berytos (Beirut), that formed around the cult of Poseidon. Richly decorated with statues of Greek style, this building was laid out around a rectangular courtyard with a cistern where a dedication indicates the activities of these traders: "The association of Poseidoniasts of Berytos, traders, shipowners and warehousers, has consecrated the building, portico and furniture to the ancestral gods." Other dedications tell of Alexandrians and Tyrians practising the same occupations. And so it is through both the realm of business and the realm of religious practices that the identity of this cosmopolitan population, now frequenting Apollo's island, can be understood. In the Inopos District, overlooking the theatre, a number of foreign sanctuaries arose alongside the traditional deities of the Greek pantheon. The introduction of the cult of Serapis, as early as the third century, shows that Delian (34)

society, like other Greek city-states, was caught up in the growing popularity of this Greco-Egyptian deity from Ptolemaic Egypt. From the 180s, one of the sanctuaries to him, the Sarapeion C ⑩⑩, came under the official responsibility of the Delian *hieropoioi* who oversaw its upkeep. The cult of Isis, long known in Greek religion, was connected with the worship of Serapis on Delos, and with the cults of the Egyptian god Anubis and of Harpocrates, the Greek version of the Horus the Child.

At the other end of the terrace from the three Egyptian sanctuaries stood that of the Syrian deities Atargatis and Hadad ⑨⑧. As the dedications of the mosaics reveal, the donors who enabled the construction and development of these buildings bore Greek names (Midas, Phormion, Philippos), but they may have been Hellenized Orientals. Although the cults

were very probably related to the progressive settlement on the island of traders from Egypt and the Levant, the dedications and the lists of subscribers attest to the very varied ethnic origins of the faithful. The deities themselves are often referred to in the Delian inscriptions by their Greek equivalents (Aphrodite for Atargatis, Poseidon for Baal) or by juxtaposition of their Greek and oriental names (Isis Astarte, Zeus Hadad).

Roman tutelage, then, was not immediately perceptible on Delos because Rome's policy in the second and first centuries, as elsewhere in the eastern Mediterranean, was based on intermediaries: the Attalid kings and the Greek city-states of Athens and Rhodes. However, the presence of Italians was evident in the first century. The people who called themselves "Italici" were grouped into "colleges" whose delegates (*magistri*) held, in the inscriptions, the titles of Hermaists, Apolloniasts and Poseidoniasts, designating the cults around which they formed. The Competaliasts, devoted to the cult of the *lares compitale*s, brought together freedmen and slaves involved in the business dealings of Italian firms with branches on Delos. The *lares compitales*, the deities that protected crossroads, were celebrated outside the doors to Italian houses, as shown by the many painted shrines that can be seen in the residential districts, in the Agora of the Hermaists and Competaliasts, and among the monuments dedicated to the cult of the *lares* in the centre of the square. On the square (2), several bilingual inscriptions set out, in Greek and Latin, the lists of Italian donors who had been members of these colleges and paid for the offering of a statue.

Other dedications specifically mention an association of Roman shipowners and traders that seems to have run its business through branches in Delos and Alexandria.

The world of finance and banking was also very well represented in the inscribed monuments of Delos, with Italians and Orientals chiefly featuring. On the approaches to the Agora of the Delians (84) and along the way leading to the propylaea (5), several dedications are evidence of honorific statues presented by trading customers to Italian bankers practising on Delos.

Like the Orientals, the Italians had a clubhouse that was very prominent within the sanctuary, probably in keeping with the economic and financial power they wielded on the island. Referred to by archaeologists as the "Agora of the Italians" (52) because it was laid out like a square lined with porticoes and monuments, it was above all a meeting place for the Italian community of Delos. To concede this huge plot to them in the final third of the second century, the Athenian administration clearly had no qualms about hiving off part of Leto's sanctuary that stood close by. Whereas the vast central space could be used for commercial activities and assemblies, the monuments lining it attested to the social and occupational spheres in which its occupants moved.

The building was fitted out through the generosity of a number of donors, whose identity reveals the activities of this powerful community. As shown by (36)

the inscription on the architrave (*ID* 1717), the colonnade of the northern
part was presented by one Philostrates of Ashkelon, from Palestine, who bore
the title of "banker on Delos" on many monuments. These monuments were
funded either by him for his family, or by his Italian clientele to honour him,
and the dedication on one of them, found in a house that was probably the
banker's own, shows that he was made an honorary citizen of Neapolis (Naples).
Statues of Philostrates and his sons adorned one of the niches located behind the
colonnade, as attested by the dedicatory inscription found on the site (*ID* 1722):
"The Italians dedicated the statue of Philostrates, son of Philostrates, banker on
Delos, and his sons, because of his equity and his generosity, to Apollo."
The west colonnade, for its part, owed its construction to Caius Ofellius Ferus,
another influential Italian and member of the Ofellii family of Campania. The
colossal statue as an athlete that the Italians dedicated to him in return, the work

(39)

of two Athenian sculptors, can be seen in Delos Museum and the dedication on its base indicates where it stood on the site.

Several other niches contained honorific statutes recording the benefactions of political figures, like Quintus Pompeius Rufus, consul at the same time as Sulla, and works of art by renowned sculptors, like the Pergamonian statute of the Fighting Gaul, housed in the National Archaeological Museum, Athens and found in one of the niches of the northern part.

Delos and the free port: governing without a city-state

After losing its independence in 167, Delos was no longer a city-state but an astonishing cluster of communities bound together by shared activities and decisions.

In the business world, Italians and Orientals were associated. While the Italians were tied to Philostrates of Ashkelon, the Poseidoniasts of Berytos granted very great honours to the banker Marcus Miniatus. Many inscriptions also attest to marriages uniting Phoenician and Italian families. In the gymnasium (76),

(40)

young Phoenicians, Italians, Athenians and Greeks of all origins joined in athletic exercises and served their *ephebia** together. The only criterion for admission was that they should be free-born. In addition to their own cults, all took part in tributes to Apollo but also to the goddess Rome, celebrated from 167 onwards at the festival of the *Romaia*, as in many other city-states of the Greek world. Following a deep-rooted habit in Athenian institutions, the Athenian community on Delos adopted as of 167 the cleruchy as its model, an extension of the city-state of Athens, in the organization of its government. Decisions were taken at assembly and by decrees, beginning with the wording "The Council and People of the Athenians residing on Delos". The Hellenized communities replicated this institutional arrangement: the Phoenician associations of Tyre and Berytos met in assemblies and voted on decrees which were worded manifestly in imitation of the Athenian documents. One of them specified that the assembly of the Herakleistes of Tyre was held in

(41) the sanctuary of Apollo, possibly in the former *ekklesiasterion* of the Delians of the classical period and the period of Independence (47). As evidenced by many dedications to be seen on the site, including that in honour of the *epimeletes* Theophrastos, some decisions were taken conjointly by these different communities, "the Athenians residing in Delos and by the Romans and other foreign merchants and shipowners resident in Delos" (*ID* 1645). This should probably be seen as a sign of Athens' waning power on Delos: although the city-state maintained the office of administering the sanctuary and the territory, economic and financial power was just as much in the hands of Italians and Orientals who must have exercised their rights, even if it is not known what institutional changes there might have been on the island during this period.

Primarily it was Rome that remained the real decision-maker and that exercised its tutelage over all local activities. A long Athenian decree for the guidance of the *epimeletes* Ophelas, dated 147–146 and discovered on Delos, laid down that the tasks of administration of Apollo's island were in the service of "citizens of Athens, [of] their children and [of] their womenfolk, the Roman people and other peoples that were friends and allies" and that they should "abide by the decisions of the Roman Senate and the instructions conveyed by the embassies". Roman control must have been exercised all the more over the Athenian magistrates of the period because the Peloponnese was (42) at that time engaged in a struggle against Roman rule.

Two dedications, one in front of the portico of Philip V (3) and the other in the Agora of the Delians (84), show for that matter, probably as the result of a Roman decision, the reappearance of Delians on the island in the late second century. The authors refer to themselves as *Delioi* in paying tribute to two high-ranking Roman magistrates: Marius Antonius, quaestor in the East in 113 and Gaius Julius Caesar, father of the dictator, proconsul in Asia in the early first century, referred to in Latin as "patron". Some of the descendants of the Delians expelled in 167 must have obtained the right from the Roman authorities to settle again on the island. Two Delians even contributed to constructions in the Agora of the Italians (52).

A Brief History of Delos

Delos and war in the first century

By the late second century, Rome had put an end to the Hellenistic kingdoms and largely dominated the eastern Mediterranean, while conducting an active

diplomacy with the Lagid kingdoms whose sovereigns were under its sway. A movement contesting Roman rule developed in the first century at the instigation of King Mithridates VI of Pontus. He saw himself as the defender of Hellenism against Rome and the movement found a considerable echo with the populations of Greece and Asia Minor whose city-states reeled from the repercussions of Roman conquest, including through the taxes levied by the new ruling power. On Delos in the late second century were a number of dedications from this Pontic king who saw that Apollo's island enjoyed his liberality. In 88, Mithridates took hold of all of western Anatolia, where he set himself up as a liberator, and Greece, which he then invaded, rallied to him. Athens itself, after much debate, opted to support him. Amid a climate of hostility towards Rome, shared

(43)

by a majority of Greeks, Mithridates ordered the slaughter of the Italians: this decision led to a bloodbath in Asia Minor and in two cities with large Italian communities, Ephesus and Delos.

Delos has been spared from war throughout its history. In the recent crises of the Hellenistic kingdoms in the face of Roman conquest, it had been protected, as in the past, by its sacred status and by its economic and commercial role. The Mithridatic war brought unprecedented violence to Apollo's island of a kind

that deeply divided the community of interests that had formed there. That the Athenians rallied to Mithridates clearly showed, besides, that in the early first century the commercial and financial interests of cosmopolitan Delos benefitted only a minority of families of note. The participation, at least in Asia Minor, of Greek populations in the massacre of Italians was also evidence of the climate of resentment and hatred fostered by the economic power of western populations settled in the eastern Mediterranean and by Roman taxation.

The consequences of this serious crisis were dramatic for Delos, which saw the collapse of the system on which its prosperity was based. The troops of Mithridates led by Archelaus, crossing the Aegean Sea from Asia Minor to Greece in the autumn of 88, ransacked the island slaughtering the Italians. This catastrophe led to the departure of many oriental traders and financiers who lost their partners and their property there. The traces remain of the destruction of the gymnasium and of the fires in the residential districts, where upper floors collapsed. The large quantities of monetary hoards* found in the houses, made up essentially of Athenian stephanephoric coins that were the currency of commerce, indicate that the owners often did not have chance to flee with their money.

The uprising orchestrated by Mithridates was progressively quelled by Roman power which, under Sulla's command, restored its authority over the conquered lands and had the Greek city-states pay a heavy price for having rallied to the king of Pontus, in the wake of a campaign of pillage, massacre and destruction that bled the territories dry. Sulla waged war in Greece and Asia as proconsul from 87 to 85. On Delos he had a very large monument erected, of which only the marble base remains, at the eastern end of the Agora of Theophrastos (49) and

(45)

on which the Latin name of the dedicant can be read: "Lucius Cornelius Sulla son of Lucius, proconsul."

Two further fragments bearing the same titling can be seen near the portico of Philip V and may have belonged to a replica of that building. Sulla handled the interests of the inhabitants of Delos with caution and, while crushing the rebellion in Athens, left the administration of Apollo's island to Athens. Shortly afterwards, Romans and Athenians were careful to restore a number of monuments in honour of Roman magistrates, in particular the statues of Billienus, the works of the sculptor Agasias of Ephesus, raised just before the catastrophe. One of

(46)

(47)

(48)

them ㉘ stood at the north-eastern end of the Portico of Antigonos, with the Latin wording *A. Attiolenus A. f. Vel(ina) reficiundam coiravit*, "Aulus Attiolenus son of Aulus, of the Velina, took care to have the statue restored".

In the years that followed, dedications in Greek and Latin continued to associate "the Athenians, Romans and other Greeks living on Delos; merchants and shipowners", the sign of a gradual rebuilding of the economic and financial community of Delos after the catastrophe. A marble base discovered in the Agora of the Italians presents a list, set out in two columns, of twelve Italian names of Hermaists, Apolloniasts and Poseidoniasts, that can be precisely dated to the year 74 (*ID* 1758). However, some of the dedications emphasize the aid provided by some or other Roman benefactors for the island's security and defence, a sign that the Mithridatic crisis had not been entirely averted.

Indeed, the Mithridatic War against Rome drew largely on alliances with pirates of Cilicia and Crete who had set up what were tantamount to city-states. The removal of the Rhodian fleet by and large from the Aegean Sea and the disappearance of the Attalid kingdom of Pergamon also enabled the pirates to thrive. On Sulla's death and benefitting from new territorial boundaries in Anatolia, Mithridates revived his plans for territorial expansion against Rome in the year 73 and confronted the Roman generals Lucullus and then Pompey. It was against this background that the troops of the pirate Athenodoros, ally of Mithridates, ransacked the island of Delos once more in 69. It is not always easy to tell from archaeological evidence whether the destruction of a building should be attributed to the crisis of 88 or 69. But the island of Delos does not seem, this time round, to have recovered from the havoc and it ceased to be a central point for Mediterranean commerce. Several Italian families, who can be traced through honorific inscriptions, settled in mainland Greece: the city-state of Argos took in several of these traders and businessmen in the latter part of the first century.

The Roman legate Triarius, mandated by Lucullus, received numerous honours from the population that remained on Delos, who called him "saviour" in recognition. His sea campaign probably drove off the pirates effectively. He also had a defensive wall erected on Delos, several stretches of which can be seen on the site. Triarius' Wall ringed a small area including the sanctuary, the harbour and the northern district of the island, and the blocks it was made of came from ruined buildings. For the first time in its history, Delos, having experienced the devastation of war, protected itself from new incursions with the means to hand, like many small city-states of the Greek world. The sack of 69 did not cause Delos to be abandoned. A few inscriptions and remains attest to a community of Athenians and Romans, but the island lost its commercial attractiveness, while other ports in the Mediterranean, like Ostia and Puteoli (Pozzuoli), thrived.

In 58, a law of the Roman Senate and People tabled by the consuls Gabinius and Calpurnius, known as the "Gabinia-Clapurnia law", was cut on the blank face of a third-century stele on Delos. The text recalled Rome's victory over the pirates and mentioning that Apollo's island had always been "sacred, free and exempt from duties", it stated that Delos and Rhenea could not be subjected to levies by publicans. This immunity from taxation was of a kind to maintain if not revive the island's economic activities. This is attested by dedications that are identically worded in which Athenians and Romans, residents, traders and shipowners, came together to honour the *epimeletes* of the island, who were still Athenians, and Roman dignitaries. Around 45, the wording of the dedications changed, mentioning only, until the end of the first century, "the Athenian people and inhabitants of the island"; a sign that the cosmopolitan business spheres of traders and shipowners had found other havens in the Mediterranean, whereas the occupants of Delos followed the policy of the city-state of Athens.

The population, loyal to a centuries-old habit, continued to grant honours to the new masters of the Mediterranean with the ebb and flow of conflicts that shook the Roman Republic. Having voted honours to Julius Caesar in 48, the Athenians of Delos consecrated a statue to Hortensius, the uncle of Brutus, in 43, then to Octavian, the future Augustus, in 30, and to Julia, the daughter of Augustus and wife of Agrippa, in the 20s. Delian epigraphy still yields up a few testimonies of this diplomatic activity, largely based on that of Athens, to the point that the sanctuary of Delos remained a place where Athenian honorific decisions were displayed until the second century AD, with dedications in honour of the Roman emperors Titus, Trajan and Hadrian.

(49)

From Paganism to Christianity: the challenges of religion

Within the bounds of the city and the sanctuary protected by Triarius' Wall, houses of the imperial period were built over the Hellenistic ruins. The remains can be clearly seen in the ruins of the Hypostyle Hall (50). A little further on, the Minoe fountain (30) is encompassed within a house. In the mid-fourth century AD, baths were constructed in the Agora of the Delians (84) and south of the Agora of the Hermaists and Competaliasts (2). Although the urban density declined substantially, settlement remained continuous in imperial times.

Several craftworking facilities, such as wine presses that can be seen in several places in the northern district, were set up where the Hellenistic city had been, indicating that activities were more rural than before. The house of Kleopatra and Dioskourides (119) accommodated a wine press and a crushing tank in one of its rooms. A Christian cross was carved on the threshold, perhaps giving a chronological indication about the later conversions of the residence.

(50)

Apollo's island continued to receive the honours of Athens. A few inscriptions of the second century AD commemorate *dodekaides*, sacrifices of twelve animals sent by the city-state. The ceremonies were organized by a priest of Apollo, with the priesthood becoming a life annuity perhaps as from the first century, possibly because of a shortage of applicants. Other island city-states, like Keos (modern Kea), were associated with these sacrifices.

This admittedly modest settlement lasted until late antiquity, as evidenced by coins of Constantine, Maxentius and Licinius discovered in a monetary hoard of one of the dwellings of the Theatre District. A marble table in a house beside the Agora of the Hermaists and Competaliasts bears a dedication to Christ that was probably one of the last Delian inscriptions. Several items of Byzantine architecture show that churches were built on Delos: the Basilica of Saint-Cyriacus, the remains of which are well preserved, can be seen at the south-east of the Agora of the Delians (86).

The island, then, remained inhabited in the first centuries of our era and maintained its status as a centre of religious life, but records are missing to explain how the small community of inhabitants of Delos shifted from the cult of Apollo to the Christian religion.

(51)

Epilogue: news in the history of Delos by way of archaeology

The exceptional wealth of Delian records from excavations, whether in the form of inscriptions, artisanal objects or architectural remains, can be used to reconstruct, with a rare precision for antiquity, the life of the communities which, down the centuries, made Apollo's island a place from which Greek civilization radiated outwards. It is this constant connection that can be made between the writings carved by the inhabitants (decrees, laws, accounts and inventories, dedications) and the monuments erected in the sanctuary that make Delos one of the most precisely known sites of antiquity.

And yet, whole swathes of the lives of the Delians remain mysterious and can only be enlightened by new archaeological research. The dwellings of the archaic and classical periods are practically unknown. The cultural connections and interactions of Delos with other sometimes remote regions of the Greek world need to be specified through studies of provenance. Examination of the harbour facilities and their chronology ought to be resumed using new technologies. The agricultural and artisanal output of the imperial period must have been involved in commercial circuits that remain little studied. And the period of late antiquity also deserves researching more fully.

Even so, the uninterrupted work on the site of Delos since the late nineteenth century has gradually filled the gaps in the picture, sometimes challenging certain established ideas. It has gone along with the publication of series of records that serve as benchmarks for research on other Mediterranean sites because of the very complete nature of the finds made on Delos. New inscriptions are regularly discovered during digs: the latest two, from the Sarapieai, were published in 2006 and 2007 and an honorific decree from the sanctuary of Apollo in 2019. The architectural study of monuments, the publication of which is in progress for the Hypostyle Hall, the Artemision, Triarius' Wall and the large commercial buildings of the west coast can be used to refine the chronology and specify the conversions of each of these building in connection with the written records about them.

The examination of tableware, from fragments of ceramic and glass found in the residential districts, has considerably advanced knowledge of the habits of the populations and of economic circuits. For example, one study has revealed the introduction into culinary habits on Delos of shapes of dishes corresponding to the arrival of new populations and contrasting with the pots for traditional stewed dishes. The study of amphoras through statistical analyses accounts for the provenances of imported wares and fluctuations in the volume of trade from decade to decade.

The role of Delos as a great Aegean economic centre has been contested because of the apparent inadequacy of its commercial infrastructure. Exploring this issue, an architectural analysis programme has recently revealed the very large surface area for storage and commerce in the shops scattered around the residential districts and the arrangement of warehousing along the sea front, that meant that Delos, through optimizing space, had storage capacity equivalent to other great ports of the Mediterranean.

The importance of Apollo's island as a centre of artistic production at different times in its history now appears very clear from studies of sculpture, modelling and artisanal objects. Input from new technologies has recently revealed the use of polychromy on works that were thought to have had the whiteness of marble.

Although Delos is indeed an outstanding site in respect of the records that its ground constantly turns up, it can be perceived, too, from the pages of its history, that it is at the same time emblematic of the achievements, innovations and contradictions of the Greek world. It is a superb observation point for understanding the aspirations and constraints of ancient societies, as visitors will perceive when looking out from the top of Mount Kynthos over the island of Apollo and the surrounding Cyclades.

Glossary

Amphictiony: religious league of several member states tasked primarily with the administration of the sanctuary of Apollo at Delphi.

Amphictyons: name given, with this spelling, to Athenian magistrates in charge of the administration of the sanctuary of Apollo on Delos during the classical period, when the sanctuary was under the rule of Athens.

Architrave: the part of the entablature of a construction resting horizontally on the columns.

Bouleuterion: public building, seat of the city-state's Council (*boule*).

Boustrophedon: type of script where the direction of writing and reading changes from line to line, as with the furrows of a ploughed field.

Chora: the territory of a city-state.

Dromos: the way leading to the entrance of a sanctuary.

Ekklesiasterion: public building, seat of the city-state's Assembly (*ekklesia*).

Emporion: port of commerce.

Ephebia: civic and military service of young men before achieving citizenship.

(53)

Euergetism: financing of a benefaction for a community.

Exedra: semi-circular bench that could be both a seat and a display stand for offerings or statues.

Hecatomb: sacrifice of a hundred or so animals.

Honorific crown: an exceptional honour attributed by a city-state to a benefactor.

Kore, pl. *korai*: statue of a young girl.

Kouros, pl. *kouroi*: statue of a young man.

Monetary hoard: collection of coins and/or precious metals buried at the same time in the same container.

Oikos: building.

(The) Orientals: conventional terms for the populations encompassed in the Hellenistic kingdoms after the conquests of Alexander the Great.

Propylaea: monumental gateway to a sanctuary.

Prytaneion: focal point of the city-state, seat of magistrates.

Publican: Roman tax farmer and public procurement contractor.

Talent: measure equal to 6000 Attic silver drachms, or about 26 kg of silver.

Thalassocracy: name given by Greek historians to seaborne empires.

Tyrant: politician holding absolute power taken by force.

Further Reading

H. Brun-Kyriakidis, *Egyptian Cults and Sanctuaries on Delos*, Epitome 3 (2021).

Ph. Bruneau *et al.* (ed.), *Délos, île sacrée et ville cosmopolite* (1996).

Ph. Bruneau, J. Ducat, *Guide de Délos*, 4e éd. (2005).

P. Bruneau, *Research on the Cults of Delos during the Hellenistic and Imperial Periods*, (2024).

V. Chankowski, *Athènes et Délos à l'époque classique : recherches sur l'administration du sanctuaire d'Apollon délien* (2008).

V. Chankowski, *Parasites of the God: Accountants, Financiers and Traders on Hellenistic Delos* (2023).

C. Constantakopoulou, *Aegean Interactions. Delos and its Networks in the Third Century*, Oxford (2017).

R. Étienne (ed.), *Le Sanctuaire d'Apollon à Délos* (2018).

R. Hamilton, *Treasure Map. A Guide to the Delian Inventories*, Ann Arbor (2000).

C. Hasenohr, *The Italians on Delos*, Epitome 2 (2021).

J.-Ch. Moretti, « L'architecture publique à Délos au IIIᵉ siècle a.C. », *in* J. des Courtils (ed.), *L'Architecture monumentale grecque au IIIᵉ siècle a.C.* (2015), p. 83-116.

Cl. Prêtre (ed.), *Nouveaux choix d'inscriptions de Délos : lois, comptes et inventaires* (2002).

P. Roussel, *Délos, colonie athénienne*, augmented edition (2003).

M. Trümper, *Wohnen in Delos: eine baugeschichtliche Untersuchung zum Wandel der Wohnkultur in hellenistischer Zeit* (1998)

Cl. Vial, *Délos indépendante. Histoire d'une communauté civique et de ses institutions* (1984).

A Brief History of Delos

Figure captions

1. The ruins of the Theatre District (watercolour by Camille Lefèvre. Musée des beaux-arts de Tours).
2. Hellenistic statue of Artemis with the doe, Delos Museum (photo EFA).
3. Archaic statue of Leto, discovered on Delos, National Archaeological Museum, Athens (photo EFA/P. Collet).
4. Apollo's sanctuary and its approaches; general restitution (Henri-Paul Nénot, Ecole nationale supérieure des beaux-arts).
5. Apollo's sanctuary and its approaches (Henri-Paul Nénot, Ecole nationale supérieure des beaux-arts).
6. The orchestra and stage building restored (EFA/T. Fournet, F.-F. Muller, J.-C. Moretti).
7. Family exedra near the Propylaea (photo P. Karvonis).
8. A street of Delos (watercolour by Jean-Jacques Malmary).
9. The Naxian oikos (photo EFA/J.-C. Moretti).
10. The lion terrace in 1971 (photo EFA/P. Amandry).
11. Statue of *kore* consecrated by the Naxian Nikandre (photo EFA/P. Collet).
12. View of the passageway between the Great Temple and the Temple of the Athenians (photo EFA/C. Gaston).
13. Accounting record of the classical period by the Athenian magistrates, Delos Museum (photo EFA/ V. Chankowski, P. Collet).
14. Accounting record of the *hieropoioi* of the year 279, Delos Museum (photo EFA/P. Collet).
15. Acroterion of the Temple of the Athenians representing the god Boreas abducting Orithyia, Delos Museum (photo EFA/A. Hermary).
16. Hermaic pillar of the Prytaneion (photo EFA).
17. Head of a Hellenistic king, possibly Alexander the Great, found to the north of Apollo's sanctuary (Delos Museum).
18. The *dromos* and the bases of honorific monuments (photo EFA).
19. Aerial view of the Agora of the Delians and its porticoes (photo J.-C. Moretti, C. Gaston).
20. The sanctuaries of Delos: the Heraion in the foreground and the sanctuary of Apollo on the plain (photo EFA/V. Chankowski).
21. Mosaic of the House of the Dolphins, detail (photo EFA).
22. Mosaic of the House of the Masks, ensemble of the main mosaic carpet (photo EFA/P. Collet).
23. The law on the sale of wood and charcoal, discovered in the lower courses of the West Portico (photo V. Chankowski).
24. Statue of Rome personified, clubhouse of the Poseidoniasts of Bertyos (photo EFA/P. Collet).
25. Statue group of Kleopatra and Dioskourides, Theatre District (photo V. Chankowski).
26. Stephanephoric tetradrachm of Athens (BnF).
27. Restitution of the *kukloi* in the Agora of Theophrastos (watercolour by M. Fincker, EFA).
28. Warehouses along the seafront. State of remains of the three blocks (EFA, J.-J. Malmary).
29. Aerial view of the seafront from the lower Theatre District (photo EFA/C. Gaston).

Contents

Printed in November 2023
by n.v. PEETERS s.a.
Herent (Belgium)

ISBN: 978-2-86958-605-5
Legal deposit: 1ˢᵗ quarter 2024

Translation and editing of texts in English: Christopher Sutcliffe

Director: Véronique Chankowski – Publishing manager: Bertrand Grandsagne – Editorial follow up: EFA – Graphic design, Prepress: Aude Gros de Beler